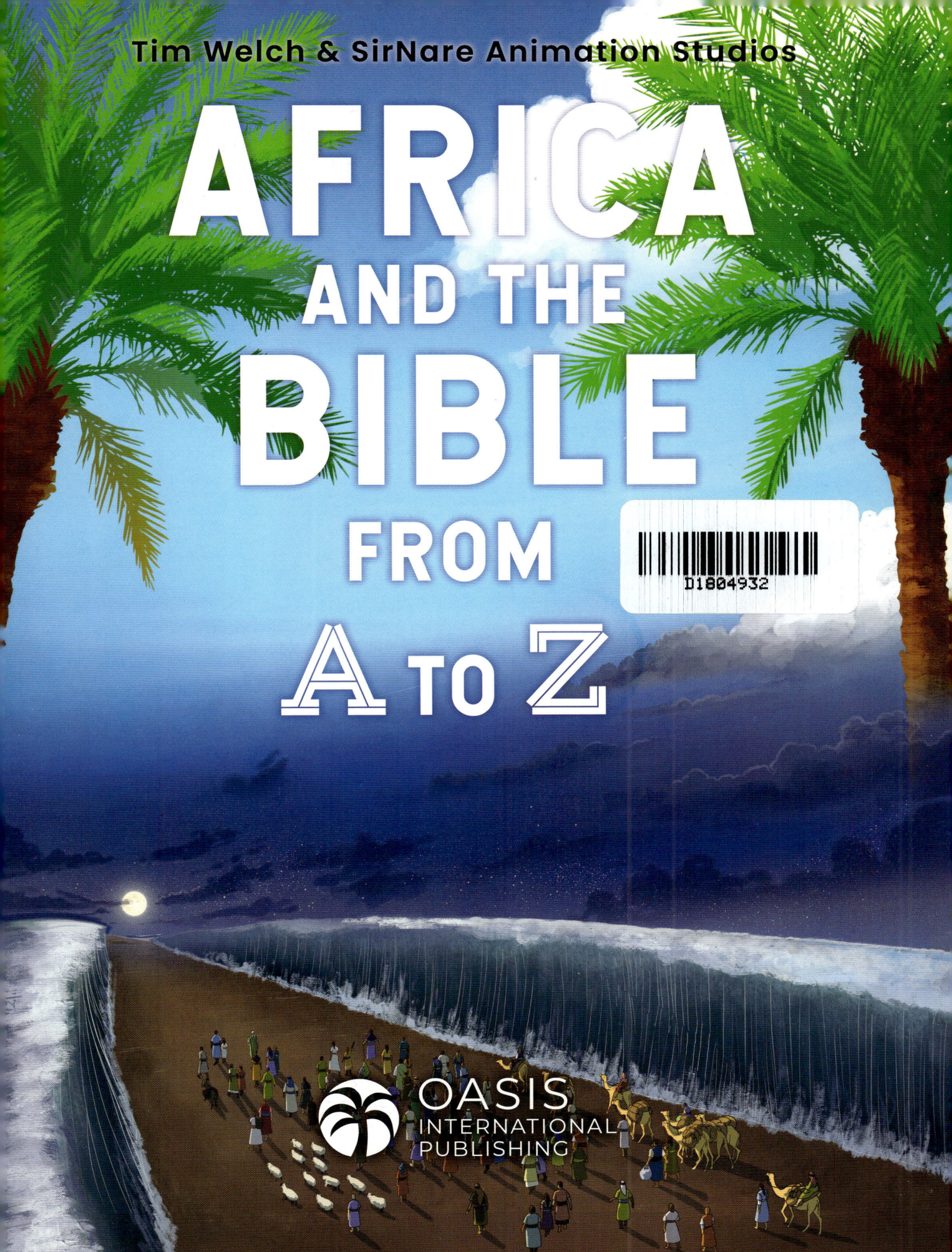

Did you know that God's story, the Bible, is also Africa's story? In the Bible God did great things in Africa. God worked through African people. God performed miracles in Africa. God made promises about Africa. Both Africa and its people are an important part of God's story. An African woman named Hagar could have been speaking for all of Africa when she said, "You are the God who sees me." Keep reading to learn how God loves Africa from A to Z!

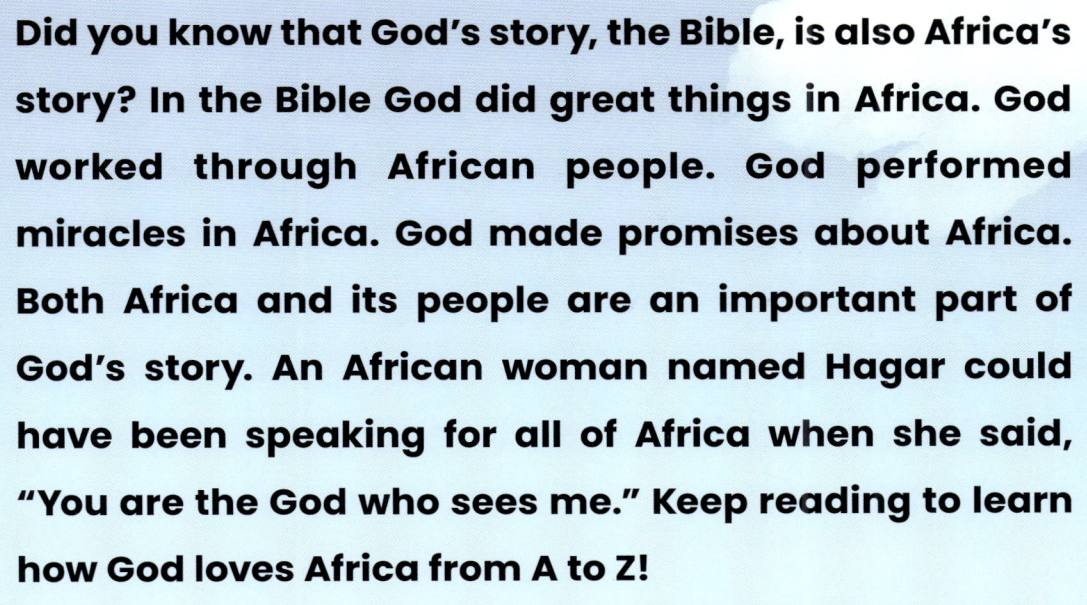

A IS FOR APOLLOS

Apollos was an Egyptian man who came from the city of Alexandria. He was very clever and knew the Old Testament well. He spoke to crowds of people to tell them the true stories he knew about Jesus. Later, two of his friends, Priscilla and Aquila, told him how God had sent not only his Son Jesus but also the Holy Spirit. He was so excited! After that Apollos travelled to Asia and Europe and taught many people about Jesus. Some people think that Apollos wrote the book of Hebrews, which is part of the New Testament. God used Apollos from Africa to help new churches grow in different countries. Someday, God may use you to help your church grow, too, or even to start new churches in other countries!

> *Apollos had been taught the way of the LORD. He spoke with great power. He taught the truth about Jesus. But he only knew about John's baptism (Acts 18:25).*

B IS FOR BIBLE

The Bible is God's Word to us written in a book. Before the time of Jesus, a group of 70 leaders wanted more people to be able to read God's Word for themselves. So they worked together to translate the Old Testament into a common language that everyone spoke. They met in the city of Alexandria in Egypt, the same African city which had one of the seven wonders of the world, a famous lighthouse.

After the time of Jesus, some people were confused about which books were part of God's Word. An African church leader named Athanasius made a list of the books he believed needed to be in the New Testament. Other church leaders agreed with his list when they met in the city of Carthage, which is part of Tunisia today. Today, the Bible has been translated into many African languages, so you, too, can read about God and Africa in the Bible.

> *Your word is like a lamp that shows me the way. It is like a light that guides me (Psalm 119:105).*

C IS FOR CYRENE

Cyrene was a large city in Libya. African, Greek, and Jewish people all lived there together. This city was known for its many writers and scientists.

The most famous person in the Bible from the city of Cyrene was a Jewish man named Simon. Simon was on the street in Jerusalem when Jesus walked past carrying the very heavy cross. The soldiers saw Simon and forced him to carry the cross for Jesus. Then they hung Jesus on the cross until he died.

Another man from Cyrene was also there that day. His name was Mark, and he later wrote the story of Jesus's life, which we call the Gospel of Mark. Simon and Mark both decided to become followers of Jesus. Jesus wants you to follow him too. Would you like to follow Jesus?

> A man named Simon was passing by.
> He was from Cyrene . . . The soldiers forced
> him to carry the cross (Mark 15:21).

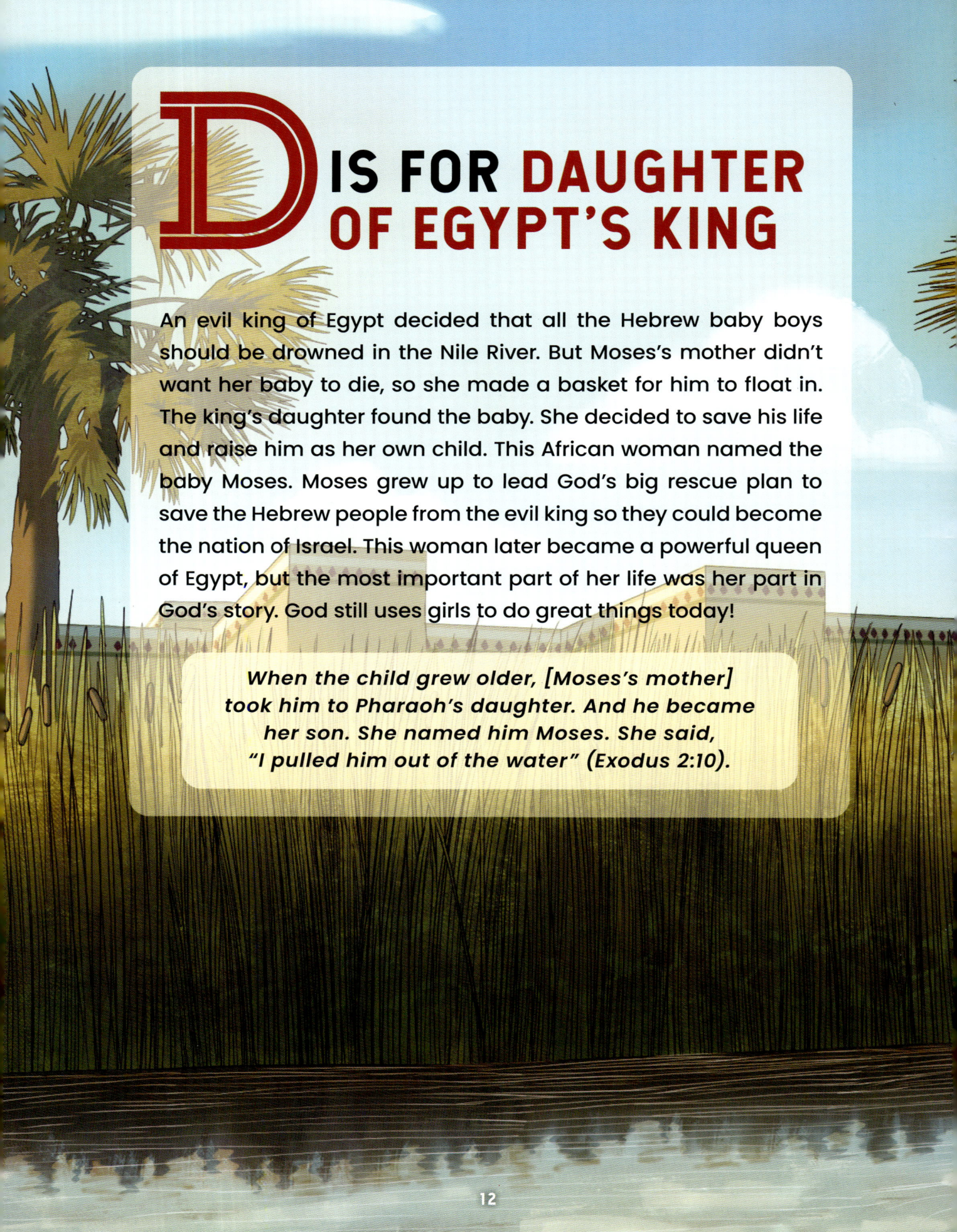

D IS FOR DAUGHTER OF EGYPT'S KING

An evil king of Egypt decided that all the Hebrew baby boys should be drowned in the Nile River. But Moses's mother didn't want her baby to die, so she made a basket for him to float in. The king's daughter found the baby. She decided to save his life and raise him as her own child. This African woman named the baby Moses. Moses grew up to lead God's big rescue plan to save the Hebrew people from the evil king so they could become the nation of Israel. This woman later became a powerful queen of Egypt, but the most important part of her life was her part in God's story. God still uses girls to do great things today!

> *When the child grew older, [Moses's mother] took him to Pharaoh's daughter. And he became her son. She named him Moses. She said, "I pulled him out of the water" (Exodus 2:10).*

E IS FOR EBED-MELEK

Ebed-Melek was an army officer from Sudan who served the king of Israel. The king's own men had taken the prophet Jeremiah and thrown him into a huge underground tank filled with mud. When Ebed-Melek learned what the king's men had done, he went to the king and begged to save Jeremiah from their evil plan. The king agreed and sent Ebed-Melek with 30 men to rescue Jeremiah. They gently pulled Jeremiah out of the tank with ropes covered in rags so that Jeremiah would not get hurt. The king's men were not happy with Ebed-Melek's rescue plan. God blessed this Sudanese officer for his bravery and his compassion. If you were asked to be brave and save someone who was being hurt – even if some of your friends did not agree – would you do it?

> Ebed-Melek went out of the palace. He said to the king, "My king and master, everything these men have done to Jeremiah the prophet is evil. They have thrown him into an empty well . . . " (Jeremiah 38:8-9).

F IS FOR FUTURE PROMISES

God made promises about the future of Africa. The prophet Isaiah says God will call the Egyptians "my people". Egypt and Israel will one day be like brothers serving the same God. Later, Isaiah says God will send missionaries to other parts of Africa. Verses in the book of Psalms tell how people from Sudan or the Horn of Africa will know God, and kings from North Africa will bring gifts to God's chosen king. The prophet Zephaniah speaks of people from all over Africa who will be God's worshippers. Many of these things are already happening. In the Bible God promises that many good things will happen in Africa! What good things do you see God doing in Africa today?

> *Messengers will come from Egypt. The people of Cush will be quick to bring gifts to you. Sing to God, you kingdoms of the earth . . . (Psalm 68:31–32).*

G IS FOR GOSHEN

Goshen is a region in Egypt near the mouth of the Nile River. It was easy to grow crops and provide food for cattle there. One of the kings of Egypt said Goshen was the best part of Egypt. When Jacob and his large family came to Egypt because of a famine in Israel, Goshen was where the king of Egypt sent them to live. They lived there for 400 years. Then the Egyptians became jealous of the good life enjoyed by these Hebrew people. Jealousy turned a wonderful land into a land of misery for the people of God. When we are jealous, it can ruin the life of others and even our own life. Do you ever feel jealous of what someone else has? If you feel jealous, what should you do instead?

Pharaoh said to Joseph, " . . . Let your father and brothers live in the best part of the land. Let them live in Goshen . . . " (Genesis 47:5–6).

H IS FOR HOPHRA

Hophra was a very proud king of Egypt. He even said that he created the Nile, the longest river in the world! But of course, that was not true. God created the beautiful Nile River. When Hophra said that, God was angry with him for telling this lie to the people of Egypt. God sent his prophets, Jeremiah and Ezekiel, to give Hophra a special message. God told Hophra that he would punish him if he didn't stop taking credit for things God had done. But Hophra was too proud to listen to God. So, God took away all of Hophra's kingdom of Egypt, but Hophra was still not sorry. Finally, God took away Hophra's life. The Bible says that God is against proud people, but he treats humble people with kindness. Have you boasted about something you can do? What if you thanked God for what he does instead?

> *Tell him, "The LORD and King says, 'Pharaoh Hophra, I am against you . . . You said, "The Nile River belongs to me. I made it for myself." So I am against you and your streams. I will destroy the land of Egypt . . . ' " (Ezekiel 29:3, 9-10).*

I IS FOR ISHMAEL

Ishmael's father was Abraham. His mother was Hagar the Egyptian. Hagar was the servant of Sarah, Abraham's wife. Before Ishmael was born, Hagar didn't get along with Sarah. After months of fighting with each other, Hagar ran away. But God told her to go back and promised that Ishmael would become a great nation. Hagar realized that God saw what was happening to her. She even called God a special name: *the God who sees me*. After she went back, Hagar had a baby and named him Ishmael, which means *God hears*. Later, Sarah had a son called Isaac, but Ishmael made fun of him. So Abraham and Sarah sent Hagar and Ishmael away again. When Ishmael grew up, he married an Egyptian woman and became the father of the Arab people. Family members need to get along. Can you ask God to help you be kind to your family even when you don't feel like it?

> *But Sarah saw Ishmael making fun of Isaac. Ishmael was the son Hagar had by Abraham. Hagar was Sarah's Egyptian slave (Genesis 21:9).*

J IS FOR JESUS IN EGYPT

After Jesus, God's son, was born in Bethlehem, King Herod sent soldiers to kill Jesus. But God had already sent an angel to warn Joseph, the father God had provided for Jesus, about King Herod's evil plan. God told Joseph to go to Egypt where they would be safe. Joseph and Mary obeyed right away and took Jesus to Egypt. Jesus's family spent several months in Egypt, maybe even a year or more. For that time, Jesus and his parents were refugees in Africa. Today, some people in Africa have to run away from their homes, too, because it is dangerous for them to stay. Jesus wants us to welcome refugees and help them feel safe, just like people in Egypt welcomed Jesus and made his family feel safe. Do you know anyone you could welcome and help feel safe?

> . . . In the dream an angel of the LORD appeared to Joseph. "Get up!" the angel said. "Take the child and his mother and escape to Egypt . . ." (Matthew 2:13).

K IS FOR KINGDOM OF CUSH

The kingdom of Cush was part of the country of Sudan. Cush had fine jewels and gold. The people of Cush made beautiful pottery, and they also made weapons out of bronze. They trained fast and strong horses to pull chariots. The men of Cush were often hired as soldiers by other kings. Cush was a powerful African empire. The prophet Isaiah warned God's people not to trust in the strength of other empires but to trust in Him. One time King Asa of Judah defeated the strong army of Cush because he prayed to God for help. God helped him and his small army win their great battle. God is stronger and more dependable than any powerful army, any nation, or any amount of money. What do you want to ask God to do for you today?

The people of Cush and Libya had a strong army. They had large numbers of chariots and horsemen. But you trusted in the LORD. So he handed them over to you (2 Chronicles 16:8).

L IS FOR LIBYA

Libya is the land next to Egypt. The Bible says that Libyans were good soldiers who knew how to use bows and arrows. Sometimes they were paid to fight for the kings of other countries. One man from a noble Libyan family even became the king of Egypt. His name was Shishak, and he attacked Jerusalem. Then he went into God's temple and stole everything. God let that happen so that the people of Israel could see how hard it was to serve a king like Shishak and how much better it is to serve God. Much later, the people of Libya began to follow Jesus. They even served him as early Christian missionaries. Today there is almost no one in Libya who follows Jesus. They need to remember how much better it is to serve God. Can you pray that Libya will decide to follow Jesus again?

> *Shishak, the king of Egypt, attacked Jerusalem. He carried away the treasures of the LORD's temple. He also carried the treasures of the royal palace away . . . (2 Chronicles 12:9).*

M IS FOR MISSIONARIES FROM CYRENE

Did you know people from Africa were some of the very first Christian missionaries in the world? Soon after Jesus died, people began telling Jewish people the good news about Jesus. But a group of Christians decided they needed to tell the Greek people too. These Christians were from the city of Cyrene in Libya and from the island of Cyprus. They chose to tell people in Antioch about Jesus. Antioch was the third largest city in the Roman empire, but many people there worshipped Greek gods. God was with the first African missionaries, and many people in Antioch decided to follow Jesus! This was the city where Jesus's followers were first called Christians. Later, the church in Antioch sent out missionaries to other countries as well. Do you know someone who needs to hear about Jesus?

> Some believers from Cyprus and Cyrene went to Antioch. There they began to speak to Greeks also. They told them the good news about the LORD Jesus (Acts 11:20).

N IS FOR NECHO II

Necho II was an Egyptian king who listened to what God told him. God told him to fight Israel's enemy. But Josiah, the king of Israel, came out to fight the Egyptian army. Necho told the king of Israel to let him do what God had told him to do. King Josiah refused to listen to him. Necho decided to fight like God had told him to anyway. Then King Josiah dressed up in a regular army uniform so that no one would recognize him as the king and he led his army into battle against Necho. King Josiah was shot with an arrow in the middle of the fight and died. His army also lost the battle with Necho. An African king listened to God, but Israel lost their king because he didn't. What does God tell you in the Bible? How can you listen and do what he says?

But Josiah wouldn't turn away from Necho . . . He wanted to go to war against Necho. He wouldn't listen to what God had commanded Necho to say . . . (2 Chronicles 35:22).

O IS FOR OASIS OF ELIM

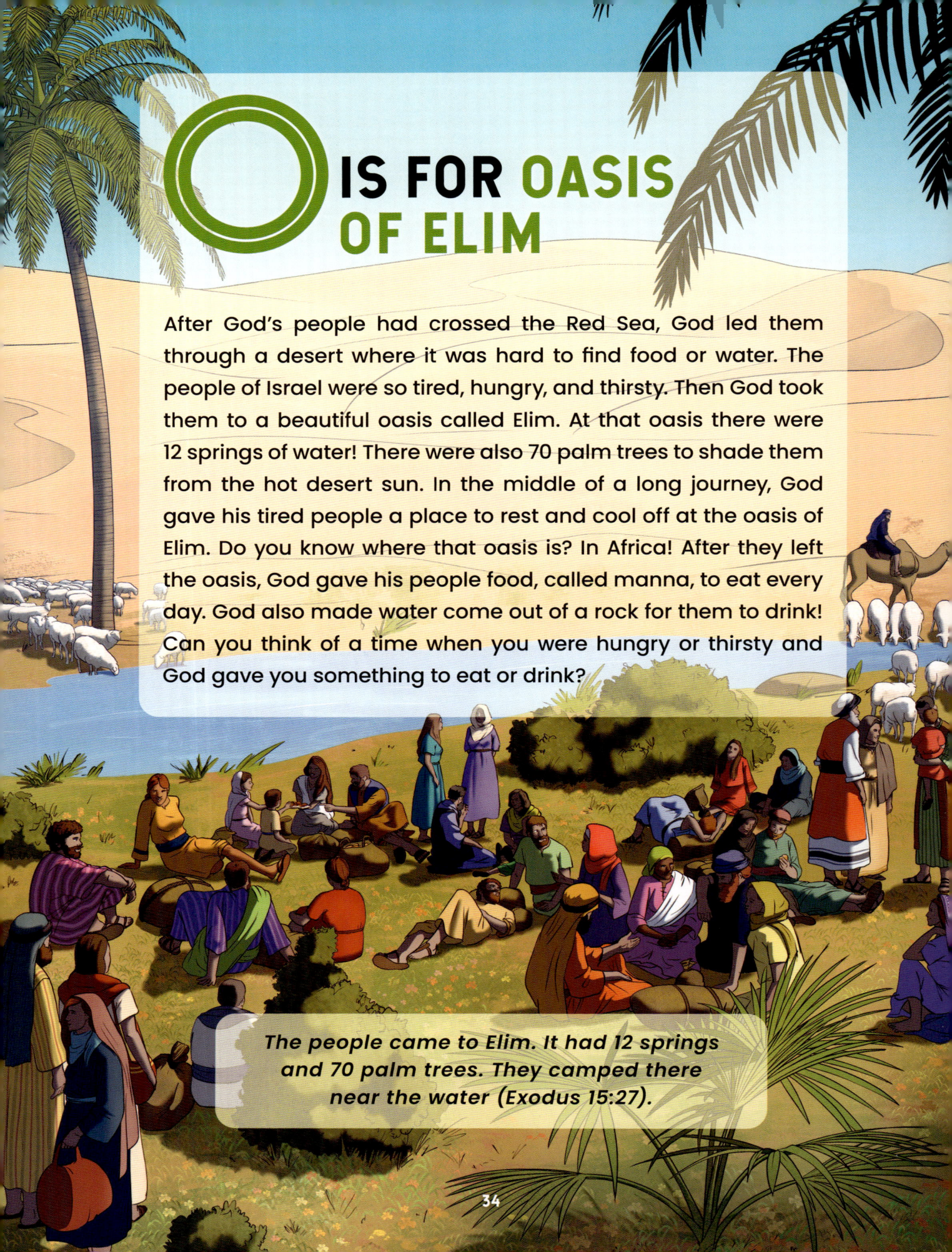

After God's people had crossed the Red Sea, God led them through a desert where it was hard to find food or water. The people of Israel were so tired, hungry, and thirsty. Then God took them to a beautiful oasis called Elim. At that oasis there were 12 springs of water! There were also 70 palm trees to shade them from the hot desert sun. In the middle of a long journey, God gave his tired people a place to rest and cool off at the oasis of Elim. Do you know where that oasis is? In Africa! After they left the oasis, God gave his people food, called manna, to eat every day. God also made water come out of a rock for them to drink! Can you think of a time when you were hungry or thirsty and God gave you something to eat or drink?

The people came to Elim. It had 12 springs and 70 palm trees. They camped there near the water (Exodus 15:27).

P IS FOR PHINEHAS

The name *Phinehas* means *black man*. Some people think he got this name because his mother came from Africa. Phinehas was the grandson of Aaron. Aaron was the high priest of Israel and the brother of Moses. One time Phinehas got angry when a group of men decided to worship Baal and disobey God in front of everyone. God sent a plague of sickness to stop them from sinning. Phinehas was the first to jump up and stop the people who were sinning. Thousands of people were saved from sickness. Another time, when the tribes of Israel got into a misunderstanding, Phinehas helped them listen to each other instead of fighting. When people did the wrong thing, Phinehas stood up for what was right. When you see something wrong happening, what can you do about it?

> But Phinehas stood up and took action. Then the plague stopped. What Phinehas did made him right with the LORD. It will be remembered for all time to come (Psalm 106:30–31).

Q IS FOR QUEEN'S TREASURER

A queen, also called the Kandake, lived in central Sudan, which at that time was called Ethiopia. She was the queen of a smaller land called Meroe. She let her treasurer go to Jerusalem for one of the Jewish feasts. On his way back home, the queen's treasurer was reading a part of the Bible, but he didn't understand it. God told Philip, a follower of Jesus, to go explain the Bible passage to him. Philip told him about Jesus and the treasurer decided to become a Jesus follower! In fact, he even asked Philip to baptize him in some water they found along the road to show that he had given his life to Jesus. The treasurer went home rejoicing. Do you have someone who can explain the Bible to you when you read it?

So Philip ran up to the chariot. He heard the man reading Isaiah the prophet. "Do you understand what you're reading?" Philip asked (Acts 8:30).

R IS FOR RICHES OF AFRICA

In the Bible, Africa is a rich land. The Nile River is the longest river in the world. It flows from two sources in Ethiopia and in Burundi through Lake Victoria all the way to Egypt. The Nile floods every year making it easier for the Egyptians to grow grain and catch fish. So Egypt became a rich empire. Genesis says Egypt was like the Garden of Eden – a paradise. Egypt and Cush had strong war horses. Cush also had jewels and lots of gold. The large cities of Cyrene, Thebes, and Alexandria were famous for their temples, libraries, and pyramids. Today, Africa still has great wealth from its animals, farms, and minerals. And it has lots of young people like you who can do great things! But God's greatest treasure in Africa is the people who love and obey him. What is one of your favourite things about Africa?

Joseph collected all the extra food produced in those seven years in Egypt . . . Joseph stored up huge amounts of grain. There was as much of it as sand by the sea. There was so much grain it couldn't be measured . . . (Genesis 41:48-49).

S IS FOR SIMEON CALLED NIGER

Simeon was an important church leader in Antioch. His nickname was *Niger*, which means *black* in Latin. Simeon probably came from Tunisia or Algeria. He was a black man who became one of the main teachers and preachers in his church. One day Simeon was worshipping God with his friends when the Holy Spirit told them an important message from God. The Holy Spirit told Simeon and the other leaders to send out Paul and Barnabas as missionaries. They listened and obeyed by helping Paul and Barnabas get ready to go on their missionary trip. They prayed for Paul and Barnabas and sent them to tell other people about Jesus. While those two men were gone, Simeon and others trained people to teach and preach God's Word. What would it look like for you to listen to the Holy Spirit and obey his voice?

> *Among the prophets and teachers of the church at Antioch of Syria were Barnabas, Simeon (called "the black man"), Lucius (from Cyrene), Manaen, . . . and Saul (Acts 13:1 NLT).*

T IS FOR TIRHAKAH

Tirhakah was a black army general who came from Cush, a region that is part of Sudan today. His brother, Shebitku, was king. Southern Israel had a king named Hezekiah who agreed that he and Shebitku would help each other. Because of their agreement, Shebitku sent his brother, Tirhakah, to fight Israel's enemy, Assyria. While Tirhakah was fighting with the Assyrians, King Hezekiah asked God to help Israel. God sent an angel to the Assyrian camp and killed many of the soldiers. So the Assyrians went back home. Tirhakah became the king of Egypt after his brother Shebitku died. He became the most important and powerful black king from Cush to ever rule over Egypt. At times African kings helped Israel's kings. Will you pray that the leaders in your country will work well with leaders of other countries to help each other?

During that time Sennacherib received a report. He was told that Tirhakah was marching out to fight against him. Tirhakah was the king of Cush . . . (2 Kings 19:9).

U IS FOR UNITY OF THE CHURCH

Did you know that Africans were there the day the church began? The church began on the day of Pentecost. Usually, it can take years to learn another language, but that day the Holy Spirit caused his followers to be able to instantly speak the languages of people from many countries, including Egypt and Libya. Suddenly, people from Africa, Asia, and Europe could hear the story of Jesus Christ in their own native language. It was a miracle! From the beginning, the Holy Spirit showed that the church is for everyone from all the different languages and cultures of the world, but we are all united as one church. Whatever language we speak, God loves it when we worship together. What languages do people speak in your church?

"Others of us are from Egypt and the parts of Libya near Cyrene . . . We hear all these people speaking about God's wonders in our own languages!" They were amazed and bewildered (Acts 2:10–11).

V IS FOR VALIANT MESSENGER

King David's son, Absalom, wanted to kill his father and become the king. He had gathered an army to fight against David's army. But Absalom got killed and someone had to give King David the bad news. The army commander knew King David might get angry, so he chose an African messenger from Cush. An Israelite man begged to take the message, too, and ran ahead. He got there before the African messenger, but he was too afraid to tell the king that Absalom was dead. When the African messenger got there, he gave David the sad news about his son. He told the truth, but he made sure his answer did not make David angry. This messenger was valiant, which means brave. He was also kind and wise. What do you think you would say if you had to tell someone something that you know would make them sad?

> *Then the man from Cush arrived. He said, "You are my king and master. I'm bringing you some good news. The LORD has shown that you are in the right. He has done this by rescuing you today from all those trying to kill you"* (2 Samuel 18:31).

W IS FOR WIFE OF MOSES

Did you know that Moses had an African wife? After Moses led God's people out of Egypt, he married a black woman from Cush. She and people from many different tribes left Egypt with the people of Israel. Different tribes and races have been part of God's people ever since! Moses's sister, Miriam, and brother, Aaron, were upset with Moses for having a wife from Cush. They said that God hadn't only spoken to Moses but that he had also spoken through them. God was angry with Miriam and Aaron for disrespecting Moses and his wife. God punished Miriam for her angry words towards her brother who was God's chosen leader for Israel. God wants family members to get along and to respect each other. What would you say if your brother or sister wanted to marry someone from another tribe?

> **Miriam and Aaron began to say bad things about Moses. That's because Moses had married a woman from Cush (Numbers 12:1).**

X IS FOR EXODUS FROM EGYPT

The word *Exodus* means *to leave*. God sent Moses to help the Hebrew people leave Egypt, where they were slaves. God heard their crying and wanted to set them free. But the evil king of Egypt refused to let them go. So God sent 10 terrible plagues, and finally the king changed his mind. But the minute they left, the king of Egypt chased after them with his army! The people were trapped between the army and the Red Sea. But God opened up a dry path right through the middle of the Red Sea so the people of Israel could walk across safely! When the Egyptian army tried to follow them, the water closed over them, and no one was left to hurt God's people. This amazing miracle happened in Africa. Do you need God to help you? He can make a way when things seem impossible!

> *The people of Israel went through the sea on dry ground. There was a wall of water on their right side and on their left (Exodus 14:22).*

Y IS FOR YHWH

One day, Moses was watching sheep at Mount Sinai in Africa. Then, he saw a bush that was covered with fire, but it wasn't burning up! God's voice spoke from the bush. He told Moses that he was Israel's God and the people of Israel were his special people. God told Moses his own special name, YHWH, which means that God has no beginning and no end. This name for God is so special that even in our Bibles today, when we mean YHWH, we use the word LORD for God.

The name YHWH was found carved on the stone of a 3,400-year-old temple in Sudan. This stone is the oldest example in the world of the name YHWH. The Bible promises that one day, the whole world will know God's name of YHWH and worship him. What are some ways that you and your family worship the LORD, YHWH?

> *The LORD will be king over the whole earth. On that day there will be one LORD. His name will be the only name (Zechariah 14:9).*

Z IS FOR ZEPHANIAH

Zephaniah was a prophet whose father or grandmother was a black African. He wrote a book in the Bible that said God would punish the world – including Africa – for its sin. But one day, people from all tribes and nations would bring offerings to God and serve him together. Zephaniah said God had a special promise for all of Africa. God promised that someday people who worship him would be found even farther south and farther west than the many rivers of Cush. Even in Old Testament times, God promised to help the people of Africa become his followers. That promise applies today to all of Africa! Today, more Christians live in Africa than any other continent in the world!

> But then I will purify what all the nations say. And they will use their words to worship me. They will serve me together. My scattered people will come to me from beyond the rivers of Cush . . . (Zephaniah 3:9-10).

God loves Africans. And many Africans love God too. For more than 3,000 years, many African ancestors have followed the God of the Bible. People from North Africa followed Jesus in the early days of the Christian church. Ethiopians also did soon after that. Christianity has grown like a strong tree in good African soil since its very beginning. These ancestors are a good example for us. When you follow Jesus, you are part of a long history of African men, women, and children who followed the God of the Bible!

A NOTE TO ADULTS

After children read this book, they may want to follow Jesus just like the African people in this book. We encourage you to make sure they understand that they are made and loved by God, that their sin separates them from the relationship God longs to have with them, that they need Jesus to save them from their sins, and that Jesus will faithfully help them grow over time into the person God created them to be. If that is the next step that they want to take in their faith journey, we have suggested a possible prayer of salvation to pray with them. After saying this prayer, we encourage you to help the children become involved in a local church where they can continue to grow in their faith and learn more about the Bible and how to follow and obey Jesus.

A PRAYER TO FOLLOW JESUS

Dear God,

Thank you that you made me and you love me. I'm sorry for doing and saying things that hurt other people. I know that hurts you because you made them too. Please forgive me for these sins. I believe that when Jesus died on the cross, he took my punishment so I could be your child. Thank you that because of Jesus, I am part of your family. Thank you that I don't have to be afraid of death because I will go heaven when I die. Please come into my heart and help me to love you and other people. Make me the person you created me to be. Amen.

READ MORE IN YOUR BIBLE

Who was your favourite character in this book?
Which places sounded cool?
Explore their full stories in your Bible!

A – Apollos
Acts 18:24–19:1; 1 Corinthians 3:4-9

B – Bible
Deuteronomy 32:47; Joshua 1:8; Psalm 19:7-11; 119:105; Matthew 4:4; John 5:39; 2 Timothy 3:16; 2 Peter 1:19-21; 3:2

C – Cyrene
Mark 15:21; Acts 2:10; 11:20; 13:1

D – Daughter of the King of Egypt
Exodus 2:1-10; Acts 7:21; Hebrews 11:24

E – Ebed-Melek
Jeremiah 38:1-13; 39:15-18

F – Future Promises
Isaiah 11:11; 19:18-25; 66:19; Psalm 68:31; 72:10; 87:4; Zephaniah 3:9-10

G – Goshen
Genesis 45:10; 46:28-34; 47:1-6, 27; 50:8; Exodus 8:22; 9:26

H – Hophra
Jeremiah 37:5-11; 43:5-13; 44:30; Ezekiel 17:17; 29:2-10; 30:20-26: 32:2-16

I – Ishmael
Genesis 16:1-16; 21:8-21

J – Jesus in Egypt
Matthew 2:13-21

K – Kingdom of Cush
(Some Bibles refer to Cush as *Ethiopia*, but it is the place we call Sudan today.)
2 Chronicles 14:9-13; 16:8; Job 28:19; Isaiah 45:14; Jeremiah 46:9; Nahum 3:9

L – Libya
2 Chronicles 12:1-9; Isaiah 66:19; Nahum 3:9; Acts 2:10; 11:19-21